In this series –

RUMI READINGS
FOR
MENTAL HEALTH

RUMI READINGS
FOR
MENTAL HEALTH

JALALUDDIN RUMI

The Scheherazade Foundation

The Scheherazade Foundation CIC
85 Great Portland Street
London
W1W 7LT
United Kingdom
www.SF.Charity
info@SF.Charity

First published by The Scheherazade Foundation CIC, 2025

RUMI READINGS FOR MENTAL HEALTH

© The Scheherazade Foundation

The Scheherazade Foundation asserts the right to be identified as the Author
of the Work in accordance with the Copyright, Designs and Patents Act 1988.

A CIP catalogue record for this title is available from the British Library.

ISBN 978-1-915311-84-9

Introduction

Jalaluddin Rumi was born in Balkh, Afghanistan, in the year 1207, and died in Konya, Turkey, in 1273.

During the sixty-six years spanning this pair of dates, he produced a range of extraordinary work in Persian which, today, is classed as 'Sufi Mysticism'.

In the seven and a half centuries since his death, Rumi's corpus, which includes *The Masnavi* and *Fihi Ma Fihi*, has been circulated widely across the Near East, the Arab world, and Central Asia.

Generations of students continue to commit selections of the 60,000 verses to heart, and allow Rumi's way of thought to permeate through all areas of their lives.

Although Orientalists venturing eastward from Europe in the 1700s occasionally made note of Sufi Mysticism, they tended to witness it through the more theatrical frills – such as 'whirling dervishes' – rather than through a deep appreciation of the texts.

It wasn't until the close of the nineteenth century that the first wholescale translations of Rumi's written work began to appear in Europe.

Even then, they remained very much the purview of a few academics, whose translations were – even for the time – laden with indescribably floral and cumbersome prose.

Although in the Occident, students would find themselves scrutinizing Rumi's corpus, it wasn't until more recently that accessible appreciations of his work became available.

A few years before his death, I asked my father – the Sufi scholar and thinker Idries Shah – for his thoughts on Rumi's legacy in the West.

Sitting in his favourite chair, a porcelain cup of green tea in hand, he looked at me hard.

'I never cease to be amazed,' he said.

'Amazed by what?'

'By the way people don't take what's perfectly packaged, and ready and waiting for them, but rather obsess with something else.'

'With what?'

'With endless and nonsensical trimmings, trappings, and paraphernalia.'

My father sipped his tea.

After a moment of silent thought, he continued:

'Read Rumi in the original Persian,' he said, 'and so delicate are the verses that you have tears rolling down your cheeks. Yet here in the West, it's served up as something submerged in a thick, glutinous gravy, so much so that its utterly inedible.'

I reminded my father that a series of publications had recently found their way to press – publications that presented Rumi's couplets in an utterly new way.

Stripped bare of what my father had referred to as 'gravy', they were light.

Indeed, they were lighter than light.

My father rolled his eyes at the thought.

'In any other place, and at any other time,' he said, 'people would be up in arms. Or, if they weren't, they'd be laughing until their sides split. Imagine it – Western poets with absolutely no knowledge of the original Persian text touting new, bestselling editions of Rumi's work! It's what we call "The Soup of the Soup of the Soup".'

In the years since my father's death, Occidental society has been flooded with all things Rumi.

Couplets ascribed to him are read solemnly at weddings across the United States, Europe, and beyond.

Wisdom drawn from his poetry is tattooed daily over the backs and limbs of Hollywood A-listers.

But the precious words uttered at weddings, tattooed into skin, and quoted in abundance, hold little or no bearing to the original verses of Jalaluddin Rumi.

So, there it is…

The great Sufi Master's wisdom available:

(a) in a form that's unreadable because it's all covered in glutinous gravy, or

(b) in another form that's completely distorted – the Soup of the Soup of the Soup.

One thing that *is* evident is that the West can benefit enormously from a clean, clear rendition of Rumi's thinking – as the East has done over the last seven hundred years.

For this reason, we have commissioned entirely new translations, gleaned in particular from *The Masnavi*. Selected and translated by native Persian-speaking scholars, the emphasis has been on maintaining the lightness of Rumi's poetry.

In an age of relentless speed and digital overload, and so as to allow the work to be accessed by those who may benefit from it most, we have arranged a series of bite-sized morsels by way of theme.

We encourage you to do what students, scholars, and ordinary people have done across the East for centuries...

To pick a single couplet, or a handful – and to read them over and over, allowing them to seed themselves in your mind.

Little by little, having taken root, they will blossom and bear fruit.

Tahir Shah

How to Use This Book

Rumi Readings for Mental Health

This book is not a treatment plan, a diagnosis, or a list of instructions. It is a companion – a book made not just to be read, but to be felt. Its purpose is to offer you moments of stillness, clarity, and comfort amid the often invisible storms of the mind.

It is a quiet guide in times of emotional difficulty. A light touch on the shoulder when things feel heavy. A mirror for the inner world – that vast, complex terrain that so often goes unseen.

These are the words of Jalaluddin Rumi, drawn from his original Persian texts and translated with care by The Scheherazade Foundation. Each quote has been selected to speak gently and directly to the themes of emotional wellness, inner resilience, self-understanding, and peace.

Whether you are living with anxiety, navigating depression, recovering from emotional pain, supporting someone you care about, or simply trying to feel more at home within yourself – this book is for you.

A Safe Place to Return To

Mental health is not a straight line. It twists, turns, loops back. Some days are easier. Some are not. The mind can be loud or dull. The heart can feel fragile. The soul can go quiet.

This book is designed to be something you can return to on *any* kind of day.

It is a space of non-judgement, of openness. You do not need to feel a certain way to read it. You do not need to understand it perfectly. These quotes do not demand anything of you. They simply offer themselves, again and again.

Let them be what you lean on. Let them be what you sit beside.

One Quote at a Time

There are one hundred quotes in this volume, divided into ten themes that reflect different dimensions of mental health – from anxiety and emotional balance, to stillness, suffering, joy, and transcendence.

The most powerful way to use this book is slowly. Read **one quote at a time**. Let it settle. Let it echo. You may not grasp it immediately – or even like it. That's okay. You're not meant to 'get' something from every line. Some are for now, some are for later.

Trust the ones that resonate. Stay with them. Revisit them. See how they shift when you do.

When You Don't Know What You Need

Some days, you won't know what you're feeling. You'll just know you're not okay. On those days, let the book fall open. Let the quote find you. Even if it seems unrelated, read it twice. Let it work quietly.

There is no need to make it mean something. Sometimes, the quote is not a map. It's a hand reaching out.

Take the hand.

Read With the Body

We often live in our heads. This is especially true when mental health feels off-balance. The thoughts get loud. The fears run loops. The stillness is hard to reach.

Try reading a quote, then placing your hand over your heart or on your belly. Close your eyes. Ask yourself, 'Where do I feel this?' Not, 'What does it mean?' – but 'Where does it land?'

Let your body be part of the reading. Let it speak, too.

Let the Quotes Walk With You

These words are not confined to the page. Once you read a quote, carry it with you. Write it on a scrap of paper. Put it on your phone background. Whisper it before sleep.

These lines were written to move with you through the world – through hard days and gentle ones, through fear, through laughter, through silence.

Over time, they may begin to speak to you when you least expect it. That's when you know they've taken root.

Write Back to Rumi

We encourage you to keep a journal alongside this book. You might write your reactions, your questions, or your memories. You might write your own poems, your anger, your gratitude – or nothing at all. Just the act of opening the page is enough.

You don't have to 'journal the right way'. Just begin.

Share If It Helps

Some readers choose to read these quotes aloud to a therapist, a loved one, or in a support group. Rumi's voice has a way of creating space – of softening silence and making room for truth.

If sharing a quote makes it easier to speak your own truth, let it.

If sharing a quote makes it easier to sit with someone else's pain, offer it.

Healing is not always loud. Sometimes, it's simply reading one line – and breathing together.

This Book Will Not Fix You

Because you are not broken.

This book is not about becoming perfect, enlightened, or emotionally constant. It is about becoming real. It is about letting go of shame and pressure and giving yourself permission to feel, to change, and to begin again – as many times as needed.

Rumi wrote: '*In the embrace of pain resides mercy; freshness blossoms when barriers are broken.*'

This book is a place where that kind of alchemy begins.

Even if just for a moment. Even if only in the quiet.

Part 1

On the Nature of the Mind

1

Free will is undeniably granted to us;
this truth is self-evident,
as no one can deny what the senses confirm.
Authority, restriction, anger, dignity, and admonition,
apply solely to those given choice.
The whole world acknowledges
the presence of free will,
as the command is clear:
'Do this, not that.'

2

Once a person attains knowledge,
their wings and feet gain stability
and their knowledge ignites and energizes certainty.
Along the journey, knowledge is inferior to certainty,
but superior to mere suspicion.

3

Partial understanding can breed
illusion and presumption,
where knowledge shrouded
in darkness begets confusion.
Even a small step forward
may be navigated safely by one with insight;
yet when faced with towering obstacles,
however narrow, fear and anxiety may lead astray.

4

The intellect is unaware of certain profound thoughts;
it only bears the weight of God's sorrow.
Choose the path of religious devotion:
God will alleviate all other sorrows.

5

Your reasoning is admirable, O accused one,
but how can I solidify and give value
to something that has turned into dust?
We must bring together the components
under the direction of love
so that it may shine with the same beauty
as Samarkand and Damascus.

6

It is unwise and futile to search for your identity
among the chaos of 'self' and 'mine',
as this sorrow serves as a diversion
from true essence.

7

O you who have become lost in laziness
and unable to distinguish others from yourself,
'Essence' refers to something that exists independently,
while 'accident' refers to something subordinate
and less important.

8

Awareness arises from our recollection of prior
experiences;
past and future act as barriers
to understanding God.
Burn both with fire;
for how much longer will you remain
attached to them,
like a fragile stem of a plant?

9

A person with an awakened heart,
though their physical eyes may be closed in sleep,
will perceive numerous inner visions.

10

Do not speak,
for the tongue is all harm.
Why do you run towards harm?

Part 2

On Anxiety, Despair & Inner Turmoil

11

In moments of despair brought on by solitude,
the presence of a companion
can transform you into a radiant sun.
Generosity views all things as reciprocation,
and recognizing this reciprocation alleviates fear.

12

When destiny approaches, this realm begins to constrict;
even delights transform into sources of anguish.
It is said:
'When destiny approaches, it becomes limited;
vision is obscured upon the arrival of fate.'

13

This restlessness, O Majid, originated from You;
otherwise, this sea would remain calm.
You have placed this turbulence within me;
now, by Your grace, free me from it.

14

Do not let worries about sustenance
burden your heart;
happiness will elude you
if you do not remain at the threshold.

15

If the fervour of your essence causes anguish,
allow the inferno to arise
from the decree of the sovereign of faith.
In times of sadness, pursue forgiveness;
sorrow is a manifestation of the Creator's intent –
respond appropriately, then.

16

The wise savour the world's blessings, free from sorrow;
the uninformed remain deprived within emptiness.
You perceived the world through a blue lens,
which is why your surroundings appeared blue.
Acknowledge this blueness as your own blindness;
criticize yourself, not others.

17

The sorrows and troubles that burden our hearts
are like fleeting vapours
that emanate from our earthly existence.
As vapours vanish into the atmosphere,
these sorrows will eventually disappear,
leaving us with a clearer and lighter state of being.

18

When someone becomes overly sceptical
and refuses to believe anything
that they cannot see with their own eyes,
they may view even the vast universe as an insignificance.

19

You are the one who inflicts wounds upon yourself;
in that instant, you condemn your own existence.

20

Suffering stems from desiring things
that cannot be obtained.
When we no longer desire those unattainable things,
suffering disappears of its own accord.

Part 3

On Grief, Loss & Letting Go

21

The sad melody of the reed flute
echoes stories of separation.
Ripped from its reed bed,
it has borne witness to countless sighs
and laments from both men and women.

22

Longing to unveil its own anguish of separation,
the flute yearns to express the pain of longing.
Once, I was like an animal, before rising to become human.
Why, then, should I be afraid?
When have I become diminished
when facing the prospect of death?

23

The old man shakes, gripped by the pain of separation.
To describe the agony of this rift
would not scratch the surface of its true depth,
lasting even unto Judgement Day.

24

Upon returning home to your loved ones
after a period of absence,
the trials and tribulations of being a stranger
gradually fade away.
The sweetness of reunion eclipses
the struggles of estrangement.

25

Experience joy in your sorrows,
for they are the signs of reunion to come.
In this journey,
descent into the valleys is essential
for reaching higher peaks.

26

Suffering and grief serve as a backdrop to happiness, strengthening its value and making it more distinct.

27

In the embrace of pain resides mercy;
freshness blossoms when barriers are broken.
In times of darkness and cold winds,
patience bursts forth in the hearts
of those who are broken.

28

My heart is filled with sympathy for your sorrow,
even though I am a stranger to you.
Your grief comes to my heart like a dear friend,
for how else could my heart understand it?

29

Tonight, solitude weighs heavy on my heart;
I long for your presence
to share the depths of my emotions with you.
My soul is like a reed flute,
echoing with lamentations and woes.

30

The person who lacks self-awareness
due to excessive behaviour
awakes to a hunger
nothing outward can sate.

Part 4

On Pain
& Transformation

31

When He desires,
the nature of sadness can transform into joy,
and the very constraints on your feet
can evolve into liberation.
Abandon strength and embrace supplication;
mercy responds to the plea of the destitute,
O impoverished one.

32

You confront me – O cry for help, O soul of man.
Why do your struggles echo those of the fearful?
Cleanse these stains from my heart,
that I may behold the garden of the pure.

33

Bad habits take root through weak foundations;
the ant of desire has transformed
into a serpent through the act of repetition.
Eliminate the serpent of desire at its birth,
or it will grow into a dragon.

34

It is said that where there is smoke, there is fire, not light;
the glow of a candle without the candle is true illumination.
Yet even in the presence of unmistakable flames,
he denies their existence, clinging to his own rejection.

35

If fate imposes suffering upon us,
how can a kind character or gentle temperament avoid it?
When will I rise from a beggar to a prince?

36

Friends suffer as much as the soul does,
and there are no indicators of friendship amongst friends.
When does a friend's suffering prevent
them from being friends anymore?
Friendship is the brain, and pain is its skin.

37

A soul cannot attain goodness
without enduring the transformative power of fire.
Just as iron must be forged to glow
as brightly as a burning ember.

38

My friend,
endure the discomfort of the sting
that you may break free
from the shackles of your own Self.

39

The root of all idols lies within the Self,
constructed within us like iron and stone.
This spark can be extinguished
by the waters of repentance.

40

Once again, I shall offer myself
as sacrifice to transcend into an angelic realm.
That which defies imagination,
that is the destiny I embrace.

Part 5

On Self-Worth
& Identity

41

You may understand the value of every commodity.
But if you are oblivious to your own worth,
you are a fool.

42

I understand what is permissible and what is not,
yet you remain uncertain about your
acceptability or relevance.
You discern between right and wrong,
yet struggle to ascertain your own correctness.

43

The essence and nature of the soul are revelatory: greater awareness correlates with a more vibrant life.

44

Look within and abandon fruitless searching;
search inside yourself
rather than constantly seeking validation from others.

45

A person devalues themselves,
despite their inherent worth,
and becomes confined to a lowly state.
What is the cause of their confusion?

46

Do not use fate as an excuse, young soul!
Why cast your faults upon others?
Look within to see where you have erred;
light creates movement, while shadows merely reflect.

47

If you feel drawn to the heavens,
spread your wings like a phoenix.
But if you sense your inclination towards the earth,
do not resign yourself to lamentation and despair.

48

You are more than just your physical form,
and you have perceived this.
Break free from the confines of the body
if you catch a glimpse of the soul within.

49

The divine spirit proclaims: 'Do not despair,'
like a father searching for his lost son,
looking in every corner.

50

How can a stone show lush green growth in spring?
Be like the soil, and vibrant blooms
will burst forth from you.

Part 6

On Resilience
& Endurance

51

From this ambush,
no one escapes impatience and haste;
patience itself serves as the tool
and method for foresight.

52

Endure the divine trial
until I sever your throat as I did Ishmael's;
I will decapitate you,
yet this is a head that, in death, finds liberation.

53

Persist in your efforts to untangle the knot, Seeker,
for a tough knot rests upon an empty bag.
As you labour to unravel these threads, you age;
seek to unravel a different knot,
a knot tightly wound around your neck.

54

In times of darkness and cold winds,
patience bursts forth in the heart of those who are broken.
The elixir of life, the cup of ecstasy:
these treasures lie hidden in the depths of adversity.

55

I advised not to associate
with those bearing sadness and sorrow,
but to seek out the company of those who bring joy
and serenity.

56

The plea of the desperate yearns for meaning;
the lament of the misled is merely an affectation.
Wherever pain exists, the remedy is directed;
wherever a boat is present, water converges.

57

Exercise patience
and keep your focus on the door;
those who wait with anticipation
will seize both opportunities and fate.

58

A Sufi is said to embody the present moment,
yet the truly enlightened transcends
the constraints of time and societal norms.
Their state relies on determination and purpose,
sustained by the vitality of a Christ-like spirit.

59

Remain quiet, like the stillness of the ocean;
do not talk excessively, like a stream.
The ocean, in all its quietude,
will then come to you.

60

Gratitude strengthens you,
while ingratitude diminishes your blessings.

Part 7

On Solitude,
Silence & Reflection

61

Silence now, that the king may address us.
Do not barter this blossom with your melody.
This flower is expressive, vibrant, and strong.
O nightingale,
be silent and rejoice.

62

The discerning choose solitude,
for it purifies the heart.

63

The monarch perceives the manifestation, as do others;
yet, once on his own, it is for the cherished king alone.
The curse of perception lies in its habitual nature;
cleaning blood with blood is both impossible
and nonsensical.

64

If everyone could see the heart's hidden anguish,
fewer would suffer in silence and despair.
Share your story, let it heal;
speak your tale, let wounds be real.

65

Thus, the soul,
bereft of trust in mind and heart,
languishes in solitude,
consumed by suffering,
and left behind.

66

If someone is not worthy of these words and prayers,
then the appropriate response to a fool,
Your Majesty, is silence.
The heavens themselves respond in silence,
as if acknowledging this wisdom.

67

The wise individual contemplates existence
and its elements,
reflecting on the destinies of
the Pharaohs and the people of 'Aad.[1]

---

1   An ancient Arabian tribe, mentioned in the Qur'an, destroyed by a storm
    after rejecting monotheism.

68

I urged my own heart:
Strive to find that magnificent reflection,
turn your eyes towards the vast ocean;
the stream alone is not enough.

69

The Source resides in the hidden
and extraordinary phenomena,
concealed from those who can only
detect immediate effects.

70

The flower's radiant petals shine like armour,
but when will the fruit within
reveal its true essence?
When the flower fades away,
the fruit emerges.

Part 8
On Love as Medicine

71

Love and compassion are qualities of humanity,
while anger and desire are the traits of animals.

72

The love we experience
liberates us from the ceaseless chatter
of psychological theory,
and the challenges of love
shield us from moral dilemma.

73

Embracing love is the path to spiritual enlightenment,
banishing suffering
and granting entry to a higher realm.

74

O heart,
you have been captivated by love,
and you are fortunate
to have discovered such valuable treasure.

75

Love, vast and limitless,
brings forth both happiness and pain,
transcending the dualities of life.
Love remains constant and unwavering,
unaffected by changing seasons
or happenstance.

76

He compromises with the opponent,
creating space for himself
in their affections.

77

Love is a subject beyond debate,
and surpasses all other matters.
It transforms conversation into a fervent plea for help.
The profound awe that love inspires
transcends verbal expression.
No one can fully grasp
the depth of this experience.

78

One who admires God's handiwork
is loved.

79

Let us immerse ourselves in pure joy
and cast away all remnants
of sorrow and distress.

80

Comfort the afflicted,
as you yourself need comfort.
Do not dwell on their sins
or reject them,
for they are already burdened
by adversity.

Part 9

On Hope, Joy
& Reconnection

81

With each moment, an idea,
like a cherished visitor,
enters your heart anew.
Embrace each thought as it arises,
welcoming it with joy and maximizing its potential.

82

Some tasks may seem challenging to begin with,
but the struggle often eases with time.
Even in moments of despair, hope remains,
and beyond the darkness
there is light to guide the way.

83

Experience joy in your sorrows,
for they are the signs of reunion to come.

84

Every time you weep, eventually there will be joy.
A servant who can foresee the outcome is blessed:
mercy triumphs wherever there are tears.

85

Speak fondly of joyful moments,
so that they may be celebrated for years to come.
May the earth and sky rejoice together,
and may our minds, souls,
and eyes be filled
with a multitude of happiness.

86

Love is the source of all happiness,
and lovers come to life through its radiance.

87

Suppress your anger,
and widen your perspective.
Experience joy, gain knowledge from others,
and cultivate wisdom.

88

Despite apparent emptiness,
there is much to discover
and appreciate with our eyes.
Even in moments of despair,
there is hope and potential for joy.

89

The joy and satisfaction
of reaching your destination
are intrinsically linked
to the hardships along the way.

90

The existence of another world
is marked by the continuous cycle
of new beginnings
and endings.

Part 10

On the Soul
& the Sacred

91

The body serves as the cradle for the soul,
like a mother carrying her child.
As a woman's pregnancy draws to a close,
anticipation builds among those around her,
wondering about the sex and appearance
of the keenly awaited newborn.

92

The souls of wolves and dogs are distinct,
whereas the souls of God's lions are fused together.

93

Once, I was like an animal,
before rising to become human.
Once more I shall shed my human form
only to soar with the wings of angels.

94

As the baby emerges from the womb,
it signals the start
of a new journey in life.
In this realm,
it heralds the dawn of a fresh beginning.

95

Some perceive death as the ultimate end,
but for those who regard death
as a gateway to a higher existence,
they will eagerly welcome it
when the appointed time arrives.

96

The flower fades away,
and the fruit emerges.
As the outer form decays,
the inner spirit rises.

97

The soul's journey is unaffected
by temporal or spatial constraints;
may our physical bodies
draw wisdom from this voyage.

98

Do not harbour anger
towards those consumed by hatred.
Hatred originates from a dark place,
and nurturing your own anger
contributes to that darkness,
conflicting with your beliefs.

99

Remembering the Divine is a pure act,
as purity emerges.
The impure shall depart, with veils lifted,
and Truth will flourish.

100

The Almighty guides the righteous
along the path of truth,
while those who embrace falsehood
are drawn towards deception.

Finis

www.ingramcontent.com/pod-product-compliance
Lightning Source LLC
Chambersburg PA
CBHW020450100426
42813CB00031B/3321/J